THE
EPIPHANY

DON'T WASTE YOUR CANCER

NICOLE LAWSON-WILSON
2023

EPIPHANY

Cover Illustration Copyright © 2023 by Nicole Lawson-Wilson

Cover design by Robert Sproles

Editing by Candice Love Jackson, PhD

Author photography by Wilson

Paperback ISBN: 979-8-39572-684-1

In the stillness of my moments,
it came to me…
Epiphany
-Nicole W.

Table Of Contents

Dedication

This book is dedicated to ALL who have had to face uncertain circumstances. May the epiphanies allow you to make the necessary adjustments in your life.

———————●———————

To my Dad, James Lawson, I continue on this journey with your strength inside of me. Rest well.

The Awakening

Breast cancer awakened me.

I was diagnosed in October 2020, Breast Cancer Awareness Month, with Invasive Ductal Carcinoma in Situ (DCIS) in two areas of my right breast. Cancer is a disease caused by an uncontrollable division of abnormal cells in a part of the body, a malignant growth, or a tumor. For the first time in a long time, I had to depend on other people besides God to help me. I have always been a giving person, so this position had me feeling more vulnerable than I ever imagined. The breast cancer diagnosis shook me to my core. I was an emotional wreck, and you could see the emotions all over my face. My smile turned into a blank face. I was emotionally and mentally shaken; all I could think about was death being upon me.

What if this cancer has spread all over my body?

Everything began to hurt after I heard those two words—Breast Cancer. I was aching, my chest hurt, I felt like I couldn't breathe. I returned to my apartment that day and immediately went into the bathroom. I took my shirt and bra off, and I looked at my breasts. I just looked at them, and the tears began to flow. I wanted to scream at the top of my lungs, but I was in this apartment, so I knew I couldn't scream. But I could cry. I stood in that mirror crying until my legs felt as if they were buckling. I chanted to myself, "This can't be happening to me." Not me. I walked around for the next three weeks oblivious to my surroundings. Part of me was hoping that this was all a mistake, and the other part left me wondering, "What had I done to deserve this fate?" "What was the lesson I had to learn?" Did they miss something in my previous mammograms? Did having many stressors in my life over the years cause cancerous growths to form?

The diagnosis of breast cancer made me more aware of some feelings that I suppressed over the years. Reflections of my childhood in Milwaukee surfaced, and I remembered feeling rushed toward adulthood as a product of parents who divorced during my teenage years. I had to learn how to survive without relying on or having expectations of others. My work career began at the age of fifteen, supplying both a sense of independence and financial security. Many of you reading this may be able to relate, but in the back of my mind, at fifteen years of age, my stress began.

As I questioned myself about how I have handled the stressors of life, I knew the answer was not so well. I'd learned to suppress my stress, which as I now realize is not good for your health.

Stress: ***A state of mental or emotional strain or tension resulting from adverse or very demanding circumstances.***

The breast cancer diagnosis allowed me to take a deep dive into my inner well-being and my circumstances. The way I internalized the stress of life events, in my opinion, has played an integral part in my actions and reactions to many situations. Today, I can say I'm thankful for the diagnosis and my awakening. I'm more aware of the things that create, cause, and affect the stress levels in my life.

Elevation And Pursuit

Years before being diagnosed with breast cancer, I decided to pursue a Master of Business Administration. I chose a Christian-based program and began my degree in 2017. I worked full-time, attended class one evening per week from 6 p.m.—10 p.m. and served as my father's primary caregiver as well as a wife and mom. My plate was full. I excelled in the program and chosen to be inducted into the honor society, Sigma Beta Delta. I was chosen and *completed* a leadership development institute program at my job in Mississippi as a precursor to a promotion within the company. I was hopeful and had the support of my family. All I needed was to complete my MBA, and things would be aligned perfectly.

Just as I was near completion, I suffered a great loss with the passing of my dad in 2019. After five years of tending to his care when he suffered a major stroke from which he never recovered along with his uncontrolled diabetes, which led to multiple amputations and end stage renal disease, I was exhausted. I felt defeated. I lost hope during this moment. The loss of a parent alters your life leaving you with a lonely emptiness feeling inside. I gathered myself, determined to complete my degree and finish strong. I had sat out of one class session when my dad passed because I couldn't focus. Grieving has its own process. I wanted to finish with the cohorts that I had begun this journey with, so I had to double up courses in my next session. I don't give up easily. In December 2019, I proudly walked across the stage to receive my MBA, with a 3.8 grade point average and induction into the National Honor Society. I felt like I was floating on a cloud on my graduation day, I had Mastered it!

Immediately after, I began searching for a higher-level position in my organization. I came across a Graduate Health Administration Trainee Program (GHATP) position offering a 1-year training with transition to a higher-level position upon completion. I applied locally, to Dallas, Texas, and Houston, Texas, after speaking with my family about the opportunity to advance. They agreed with my pursuit of a better position, even if I had to relocate. My daughters were now in college and my husband supported my goals. I didn't receive an interview for the local position, but Dallas called, I interviewed, and I was chosen. I was beyond excited even though I had to move. But since one of my besties lived in Mansfield, near Dallas, I knew I wouldn't be completely alone. This was going to be great! Finally, my season was due. I moved in with my bestie and her family while searching for an apartment.

The opportunity in Dallas was refreshing. I was determined to shine and make sure they knew I was the right choice for the position. I was in a group of five selectees from diverse backgrounds, and we gelled fairly well. I was living my best life. I felt good. I felt empowered to conquer my thirst for advancement. I had a purpose again, and I was in pursuit of my goal and hopeful about the outcome. I had given myself to everyone else, so now it was my turn. I was more than ready. I was determined and focused. It was a financial stretch to pack up and move, but I knew the investment would pay off. I believed in Me.

Before I go further, allow me to provide a little background information. I have worked for four years as an Administrative Officer, handling all things for a Neurology department for a hospital in Mississippi. I have either volunteered or been *volun-told* to aid in all functions of this department. Frankly, I loved it. My supervisor, Dr. Undesser was highly supportive of my efforts and has taken the time to show me the ropes and placed me with higher responsibility. His structured guidance is the reason I decided to obtain my MBA. I had never taken any business courses; I leaned toward health sciences in my undergraduate coursework.

I became my supervisor's "right-hand," but I'm left-hand dominant. I would arrive for my shift one hour early because my supervisor would be there, completing spreadsheets, replying to emails, etc. During these moments, I was able to study him and his way of doing things as well as his approach to problem solving. I became savvier with the business of handling business in the department to the point that when my supervisor would leave for vacation, he left me with the capacity to take charge. I found the role to be an adrenaline rush for me. I liked being the problem solver. I liked putting the fires out as I labeled the situations. Earning my MBA was the icing on the cake for me to step into an administrative role. And being chosen for the Dallas position gave me that high, that confidence that had been lost in the shuffle of life moments.

I prayed for guidance and opportunity. That prayer was answered while I was asleep and dreaming. I felt a rush of cold air brush across my face, and I awoke. On the same day, I got a call for the position in Dallas. And I felt the need to make this moment count. Here I am... feeling free, feeling confident, feeling like my time has arrived. Some of me felt like a young adult moving into her first apartment, some of me felt free from the routine responsibilities, and some of me missed my close-knit family. I threw these emotions into this program, and I went to work, because after this training, I'm elevating.

I had spent the last five years caring for a sick parent, juggling school, work, and life. As I loaded my car to leave for Dallas, Texas, I remember looking back in the rearview mirror at my beautiful home and my family standing at the garage. I felt saddened that they couldn't take this journey with me. A plan was set in place to physically see each other at least once a month whether I came home or they came to me. As I rode down the highway, I opened my sunroof and let the sun beam down on my face. I turned the music up loud. The drive was liberating, and I was looking forward to new experiences and my future. I wanted to add value to myself and to the organization I worked for. Investing in myself meant committing myself to being in better shape physically and mentally. I owed this to myself. *It's my time, it's my season*, I told myself. I was looking forward to being in a bigger metropolitan area with more opportunities to explore. My dreams are finally coming true. Many years ago, my husband and I had considered moving to Dallas but it didn't work out. Maybe this time, it would.

At this moment, it didn't matter to me that my family wouldn't be present all day, every day. We could FaceTime. I didn't want this opportunity to pass me by. I knew it would all work out. Living with my bestie and her family temporarily made me feel less lonely. I'd visited Dallas periodically, so it wasn't a foreign place to me. I drove down that highway on a natural high, thinking what if this all works out. I could probably persuade my husband and children to follow. They want to see me excel and be at my best. I got this. All I need to do is put in the work and the rest will follow. I'm going to let it all flow and I'm going to succeed. I had planned it all. I could see myself in a leadership position.

One month later, I moved into a one-bedroom apartment in Grand Prairie, a Dallas suburb. My husband and children loaded up a trailer with excess furnishings from our home, I purchased a headboard and mattress locally. Settling in reminded me of moving into my first apartment over twenty years prior and the sense of independence it brought. I was responsible for taking care of me again, and it felt so different.

Apartment living was an adjustment for me. I wasn't used to having people walking above my head throughout the night and strangers watching me come and go. I remained alert and kept my guard up even though I felt safe in this gated apartment community. I kept my apartment in pristine condition with decorations that reminded me of my home in Mississippi. And although I missed my family dearly, I was able to just focus on me—focus on my job, focus on my spiritual walk, re-center myself and finally pursue more goals. I found myself having more intimate talks with God, reading more and being able to listen without any clutter in the background.

It felt good to have this space and time. Although there were times I would get lonely, I tried not to burden others to accommodate my loneliness. Sometimes, after Face Timing my family, I would shed a few tears. I realized how great the sacrifice was. My ideal day in Mississippi would be coming home to my family, sharing my day at work, eating together, and spending some family time watching television or just talking. Now, I came home to an apartment—alone. I kept reminding myself that this is for a greater goal, and we would all benefit soon. At least, this was my prayer. I learned, though, that I liked my alone time as equally as I liked being around people. I needed the balance of time alone, to dream, to re-focus. The move to Dallas is working for me. My transition to Dallas was ordered. My determination stems from my desire to advance in the Healthcare Administration field, to add value to the organization and make this MBA that I earned and completed in 2019 pay for itself. I desired a better position. The job was going well, I exerted myself into many projects, accepted extra assignments, and volunteered when needed.

My second week on the job, a patient's wife sent a platter of sweet treats for me to share with the other staff and gave me a card, "Thanking" me for helping her and her husband. What I did was give my word that I would follow up to questions she asked and information she desired to know about her husband who was confined in the hospital during the Covid pandemic. Visitation restrictions were hard on patients and their families, and

I understood that being far away from my own. I had sought out the answers she requested. And I returned her call on the same day with those answers. I take pride in providing good customer service. I considered this gesture to remain true to one of my values—loyalty.

As I was making my second home in Dallas, I decided to follow-up with my routine medical care, my yearly exam with the OB/GYN to get my pap and mammogram. I carried the health insurance for my family because it was more affordable through my job. Since I was living in Texas, I wanted to stay in network, and I made an OB/GYN appointment in September 2020. I was pleased with Dr. Angalene Jackson and her staff. Dr. Jackson was very attentive, she addressed all my questions, and I informed her of my past health history. She told me that she would have my mammogram scheduled with follow-up thereafter.

The mammogram appointment began like any other, the pressing of the machine on the breast tissue is uncomfortable and awkward to say the least, but it doesn't last. I was asked to sit back in the waiting room, shirt, and bra still off. Then the technician returned stating she would need more images. I thought nothing of it, so okay here I go again, more pressing on my breast. When the technician returned and stated an ultrasound was needed a feeling came over me that something was not quite right. *Hmmm*, I thought to myself. *What is going on?*

As the ultrasound technician performed the breast ultrasound, I watched the screen, paying attention to the images and what she was measuring. Then there it was, a darker area in my breast tissue that had the appearance of a spider with its legs spread out, then one area became two areas. I had an idea of what this could be, but I remained silent, praying, and hopeful. What I haven't told you is I have a trained eye in the field of ultrasound. I am also a registered ultrasound technician. Although I had limited experience in breast ultrasound, I knew enough to see the concern on the technician's face. And I really knew it was more involved when she went to retrieve the physician, who took the probe and began to scan my breast comparing the mammogram images to the ultrasound images. Next, I was told I needed to have a biopsy of the areas of concern. In disbelief, I got dressed, looked in the mirror and proceeded to check-out and receive my next appointment for the biopsy. I walked to my car, got in, and called my husband. He told me, "I'll be there to take you." And he would arrive present and supportive. I went back to my apartment after the appointment and prepared dinner for myself—a ribeye steak with onions and mushrooms. I ate it slowly and I watched television on the sofa. I was numbed by the day's events. So numb that I didn't get in the bed that night, I fell asleep on the sofa with my arms folded defensively across my breast like I was warding off an attacker. I returned to work the next day and I shared some of the experience with my cohorts. The only guy in the group, Chris encouraged me not to worry, telling me that his wife had experienced the same issue without incident; the other ladies, Tameca, Veronica, and Stacy also expressed concern with positive overtones.

The days ahead were a blur, I hoped that I would receive a call stating that there had been a mix-up of some sorts, that they had the wrong images, anything that would take me out of the equation of needing this upcoming biopsy. I wouldn't allow my mind to go to the possibility that something may be wrong, it just couldn't be me. I've been chosen to be here, remember? I braced myself after a few days for the worst scenario, hoping for the strength to be able to accept whatever the outcome. Even though there had been no definite diagnosis at this point, in my gut, I knew. I had seen ultrasound pictures of breast cancer in my training and my scan resemblance was parallel.

The Known And Unknown

The definitive I know from having more extensive testing is two cancerous tumors exist in different areas in my right breast. Yet, the unknown poses a lot of unanswered questions. Questions like, will they be able to get all the cancer out? Has it invaded my lymph nodes? What will the new breasts look and feel like after being replaced with fatty tissue? All these questions are running through my mind causing me to have a lot of sleepless nights. I have a vision in my mind of what I want the outcome to resemble; however, as the days get closer to my surgery date, I have no idea what to expect. I can only hope I can accept the outcome and be grateful for it.

The unknown must be greater than what is already known. I know I want these cancerous tumors and any other parts of the word "cancer" to vacate my body and never come back. The initial biopsy was very uncomfortable and painful for me. This procedure was performed at USMD hospital in Arlington, Texas, the same place as my mammogram. The biopsy procedure involved injecting a numbing anesthetic into the suspected areas of my breast. The room was cold and dark, and I was nervous. The doctor reviewed the images while allowing the numbing medication to take effect.

As she began to insert the biopsy needle, I could feel everything. I screamed out, "Ouch, this is hurting me." The doctor was surprised by my response, she withdrew the needle and proceeded to give me more numbing medication. On the second attempt, I tolerated the process with tears rolling down my face. I could feel the tugging of the needle and hear the clipping sound as the tissue was extracted. After the biopsy, I could feel everything. I could feel the tumors. The tumors felt like bumps under the skin of my breast. I had never felt this before, not even when performing my monthly self-breast exams. I realize that this is real, this is the moment that I allowed myself to feel the pain that this is ravaging up in my body. I couldn't reject it. This hurt me.

I'm awake.

What people don't know about me is I'm my own worst critic. I hold myself to the highest of high standards wanting to present decent and in order in all circumstances. Confidence is the emotion that catches me off guard at times. I know my flaws. I look at my face, and I can see every freckle, every bump, every dry skin patch. Many people compliment me on my beautiful skin, but I see every new wrinkle, every new pimple, and I mask it.

I'm not always confident in my walk on my best days, so when breast cancer hit me, my confidence meter plunged. I felt like people could see the cancer way before chemotherapy and hair loss. I felt unattractive. Now, I'm facing surgery and what will the outcome be. It is the ultimate unknown. What will my husband think of all these drains and scars? Should I let my daughters see these wounds? I am sensitive about my appearance. When I feel good, I do my best to look good. I put my make-up on. I add eyelash extensions. I shine. You know, it's like going to your hairstylist to change up the color of your hair. When you leave the salon, you want to dress up and go somewhere so everyone can see your new look, color, and style. I'm usually the person who is the confidence booster, and I give a good pep talk to others. But now I need to find the right words to give myself some pep. All I can do at this moment of the unknown is trust the process. The steps of the process rattled me. I listened to and read about other people's journeys, but will my path reflect any of these experiences? It remains unknown.

As I get closer to the days of my first surgical procedure, the Big One, to remove the cancerous tumors, I feel antsy. There is something stirring in my soul. I don't know if it's nervousness, being afraid, or just want it to be over because I can't control the narrative.

Choices

The decision to have surgery to remove both of my breasts was a "No brainer" for me. I witnessed three family members' journeys through this process. I remember saying, "Well, if I ever get breast cancer, they can have both of them because I want some perkier breast anyway." Now, as I faced this same fate, I was reminded to be careful with my tongue. Although I only had cancer in my right breast, I was given all options available to me. I chose a bilateral mastectomy. The most conservative option was the lumpectomy procedure, removing the cancerous masses and some surrounding tissue. I was faced with two areas of cancer in the right breast, which, by my surgeon's assessment, would leave my breast tissue needing to be rearranged to make the appearance uniformed. The problem is once those tissues were rearranged the cancer could return in a different area of the breast.

When seeking and listening for the right options, I reached out to a few people whom I trusted and whose opinion I respected. One was the owner of the Ultrasound program I attended and graduated from ten years prior. Mrs. Gill received a diagnosis of breast cancer the same year I graduated from the ultrasound program. I knew she would offer sound advice and share informative information, straight to the point and no chaser. And she did just that. This phone call led me to another reference point of contact that had received the surgical option I was most interested in, the deep inferior epigastric perforator (DIEP) flap procedure. The process of this procedure utilizes abdominal fat to reconstruct the breast at the same time the cancerous breast tissue is removed, and my nipples could be retained with the possibility of retaining reaction and sensation to touch. The abdominal incision would require reconstruction and new placement of my navel. This procedure is one that gives the 'tummy tuck' appearance and allows your mid-section fluffiness to benefit the outcome.

I chose to have my surgery in New Orleans, Louisiana, at the Center for Restorative Breast Surgery. I chose to have a bilateral mastectomy, Deep Inferior Epigastric Perforators (DIEP) flap reconstruction procedure. As I was sitting on the exam table with both physicians, surgical and plastics, my husband looking at me, waiting for my decision, I felt a rush of heat going through my body. I was having a hot flash even though I was undressed from the waist up with only a disposable paper gown on. Everyone was staring at me like I had the answer to the million-dollar question. I wished I were here to win, but that day, I felt like I lost. If they removed both breasts, my chances lessened greatly for reoccurrence. I stated loudly and clearly to all in the room, "Take both of them because I don't want to go through this ever again." I wanted to keep my breasts, but I knew this was the better choice for me. I exhaled a breath of air after the decision feeling like I had reached the point of no return. Everything began to move fast, setting the surgical dates, instructions to prep. It was overwhelming, it felt like the room was spinning with people all around me talking at the same time, Blah, Blah, Blah. I missed much of the instruction; I just could not comprehend it all. Thank goodness they give an informational packet that reinforces everything discussed. I am convinced that a lot of patients react in this way.

I never imagined I'd get new "boobs" covered mostly by my insurance, but what will it cost *me*? What would I look like after the surgery? How long would my scars be? I admit the idea of having my breasts removed made me hurt just thinking about it. I've always had sensitive breasts, responding breasts, and I didn't want to lose that part of me. I like having breasts. I liked having one larger than the other, especially if it meant they didn't need to be removed. I didn't want to be cut open. I just didn't. One thing I was sure of, implants were not my reconstructive choice. I know they offer a perkier look, no need to wear a bra, but in my gut instinct I was against something foreign being in my body that has a shelf life of about ten years, if no complications arose. After that, those implants would need to be replaced. I'm 48 years old with a breast cancer diagnosis. At 58 years of age, I would need to replace my "tits" again and have more surgery. No thanks, I'll pass.

When I walked into St. Charles Surgical Hospital on December 18, 2020, at 4am in the morning, I was calm. I was at peace with my choice and at peace with my life. Maybe I was also in shock that this day was here, but this was my reality. But it was less of a blow than receiving the initial diagnosis. As I sat in the waiting room, I looked at my husband. I thought to myself, "he is here with me alone and if something happens while I'm in surgery, he might not be able to handle this." We were in New Orleans during the Covid-19 pandemic, so there were limited people allowed to be at the hospital. My daughters stayed home to attend school and work. I had to remain in the hospital for a few days after the surgery. I sat there. The décor in the hospital had the essence of a high-class spa, and I thought, *this will be over soon. Lord, please let me wake up.*

According to my surgeons, this procedure would be an eight-hour surgery. My breast would remain intact, minus the cancerous breast tissue, and reconstructed from my abdominal fat. My abdomen would be tucked; it was like a mommy makeover all in one. My nipples would be saved.

My surgery took over ten hours, closer to twelve hours from start to finish. I didn't have any complications during surgery according to my husband, but he stated that he started to get more concerned after the tenth hour even with the constant updates of my progress. I awoke from my surgery numb because I was given a nerve block that lasted several hours after surgery. When the nerve block began to wear off, hell yes, I was in pain. It felt like I had been hit by a gigantic boulder that was still laying upon my chest. I could barely move.

Thankfully, I had the forethought to discuss all surgical and medication options with my surgeons prior to surgery. I expressed which pain medication worked best with my body and they listened. Morphine, an opioid pain blocker, was the drug of choice. In the past, with other minor surgical procedures, I had been given

Demerol, also a pain blocking opioid, which did not work well and produced hallucinations. It was important for me to communicate with the surgeons and relay all my previous surgical history and experiences. I wanted to lessen the pain as much as possible and I desired my surgical experience to be beneficial. The morphine worked fast and effectively. I had an intravenous pump inserted that could be pushed every so many hours for some relief. I remember awakening as the medication was wearing off, feeling uncomfortable in some pain with pressure able to press the pump button, then drifting back off to my happy place, free of pain. Yes, I was high as a kite floating in the high winds and it felt good.

After several hours of sleeping and being medicated for pain, my nurse expressed that I needed to get up and walk down the hall. I thought to myself, *this damn woman must be crazy.* Here I am, cut from the top to the bottom, "my rooter to my tooter," and they want me to walk less than twenty-four hours fresh out of a twelve-hour surgical procedure. I must be dreaming. I didn't hear her say this, did I? I'm thinking to myself, *Morphine is a helluva drug, because now I'm hearing things.* There is no way I'm going to be able to get out of this bed and walk. The nurse returned and coerced me to move, to get up and begin the healing process. I complied, using a pillow to splint my stomach. With the nurse and my husband assisting me, I got up slowly, sat on the side of the bed. I finally stood up after my mind got in sync to focus on the process, which took about ten minutes, I felt unsteady and anxious at first. I lifted my foot to take the first step then the next, I walked down the hall of the hospital admiring the spa-like qualities, giving me something else to focus on while holding on to my I.V. pole with one hand and the pillow splint with the other. As I approached the nurses' station, I was given positive reinforcement by other nurses for my walking efforts, but I was so glad to get back to my hospital bed and go back to my happy, medicated, pain-relieving place.

My hope was to have an uneventful procedure and so far, this is exactly what I was experiencing. Let's see what the next days may bring. The 10+ hour surgical procedure was completed without incident. I also received a blood transfusion while in the hospital because my counts were low, stayed for three days, with one return visit after discharge, and a follow-up two weeks thereafter.

Mirror Image

I hadn't looked at myself while in the hospital, I just couldn't. However, I had my husband snap a photo as I lay in the hospital bed, so I could capture the moment.

The three-hour drive home was uncomfortable to say the least. I was padded down and wrapped up and had bulbs attached to drains coming out everywhere. I was numbed by the pain-relieving medications. I drifted into and out of sleep with every waking moment thinking, *when will we ever get home?* I was ready to be back in my comfort zone. I was a little nervous about returning home, scared of the possibility of getting an infection, or pulling one of the drains out by mistake.

When I got home, I gathered my nerves and stepped to my floor length mirror to finally take a glimpse of the new me. What I had prepared myself to be a horrific sight was the opposite. I had been given bigger breasts, not my final result, with keyhole incisions and drains of course. The breasts were initially larger to ensure viability. My surgeons, Dr. Mary Jo Wright and Dr. M. Whitten Wise at the Center for Restorative Breast Surgery in New Orleans, Louisiana, were phenomenal, in bedside manner and skill. I was swollen all over, but I could see my navel and I didn't have my mid-section doughnut flap anymore. I could see all facets of my silhouette and the traumatic experience at the same time.

I remembered coming out from under anesthesia. I heard someone with a soft feminine voice say, "She will be pleased with the outcome." When I built up enough courage to step into the mirror with drains protruding parallel on each side of my body, I was pleased with the potential results. I saw the pieces of me, and they looked the same, same color, same texture, same feel.

Three weeks after the initial surgery, I had to have my abdominal area debrided because I developed an infection. I had to have more lymph nodes removed because cancer had invaded. I lost my navel in the process. The tissues in this area didn't thrive, which, in medical terms, is umbilical necrosis, common in abdominoplasty procedures. I also found out that a third cancerous tumor was found in my right breast that went undetected in previous testing. The third tumor was found in pathology after the bilateral mastectomy. As alarming to my soul, it was to hear this news, it validated my decision to have the bilateral mastectomy as opposed to a lumpectomy. These were minor complications for me. I just wanted to heal. I was amazed at the outcome for now though facing more corrective procedures in my near future.

My hope was I could look at myself in the mirror and like what I saw. My hope was I would still be whole, feel whole, that the incisions would leave minimum scarring. I hoped for the best outcome for the uncertain fate, the unknown, the imprint that would now be a forever reminder that breast cancer had been here. After all surgical procedures, my body was tatted with the necessary lines that took away the cancer, and I have no regrets. I can now look at myself and see visible scars, visible changes in my contour, but not an unlivable nor unlikeable me. I have improved in some areas and the results give me an inner peace. I no longer worry.

Having surgery to remove breast cancer was a major life-altering decision. As a woman and married, I was concerned about the outcome. How would I look? Would I still be attractive to my spouse, or would he look at me with pity? Would I ever feel comfortable enough to take my clothes off in front of anyone again, even the doctor? These thoughts run in and out, in and out, of your mind. I recall sitting in the physician's office in Texas to get the results of the biopsy as I had my husband, Lionel, on speakerphone. When the doctor stated that the biopsy showed two cancerous tumors in my right breast, I could hear my husband gasp for breath and when he spoke again, you could hear the tremble in his voice, the tremble sound when a person is crying. Oddly, I couldn't cry, I sat in that office with a stare, unable to move, like a deer when they see the bright headlights from a car. I was frozen in my body, in my thoughts, in my expression. The doctor continued to talk and explain the next steps, but I was in shock and disbelief.

My husband had not expressed how he felt until I asked him as I was writing this book. We hadn't explored his feelings at all. His concentration had solely been on me and my outcome. He expressed that he was scared and sad when I received the diagnosis.

He said he never thought I would die, but that my recovery would be a long healing process, especially when I returned home with the large abdominal incision and drains everywhere. After all the surgeries, he thinks I look the same. His response was what I had imagined he would say although he acknowledged that he knows I'm not the same person. But I knew he was rattled after this diagnosis when I received a call from my pastor and his wife. They informed me that he had called them asking for prayer. This was not my husband's normal response, and although prayer was much needed and appreciated, the fact that my husband knew he couldn't fix it said a lot.

We all have challenges. My challenge to accept being perfectly imperfect has caused an internal fight, a real struggle to accept imperfection. I had to learn how to look at myself and feel good about being flawed in many ways. I'm not perfect. The world we live in is not perfect; no perfect people exist. I have allowed myself to let go of the things that I thought I could control and can't. I have given myself some grace to not have everything in a perfect place. I allow the imperfect me to be seen so that others know I could use some help. Honestly, I find that part of me to be more attractive. I've learned to let the flaws be what they are, noticing that people who really care about you and appreciate your journey have never even noticed the imperfections. People see the put together version that we all think is important on the outside. But, in reality, the imperfect, flawed, incisions I have allowed to be seen have drawn more positive attention than my version of wanting to be perfect ever could.

Remember, the scars will fade. Your spouse, life partner, and supporters don't care about the scars as much as you may think. The people in your life want you here, want you alive. Remember you are as sexy as you feel, and it took some time for me to feel sexy again, not because I wasn't, but because I was not allowing myself to see what everyone else saw. Give yourself some time to bounce back. The surgical procedure tightened up some areas that I had struggled with for years after having children; the outcome has been remarkable. I see an altered version of me when I look in the mirror, and I still love her.

What I Needed To Know

Although I have had encounters with others who had experienced the journey of having Breast cancer, I still felt alone to some degree. It's a member's only club.

I often left my encounters with other breast cancer survivors with mixed emotions. Being diagnosed with breast cancer can bring on emotions from the emotionless. I experienced this with three family members, my mom, my aunt, and my mother-in-law. I watched them handle the diagnosis of breast cancer differently. All three had different stages and treatments that included a lumpectomy, chemotherapy, and radiation. I witnessed the resilience of each of these women although they didn't speak about it much. I saw them continue to strive, receive treatments, and not dwell in a dark place. The common denominator expressed by all was, "I don't want to die." This statement was clear, and their strength was admired even more when I joined the members' only club.

When I received my diagnosis, I had to ingest that feeling. My heart ached; my chest tightened. It gave a bad taste to my mouth, like a dose of castor oil that I was given as a child. I disliked the taste of castor oil. Of course, my husband and daughters were the first to know. After learning of my diagnosis, I decided to come home for the weekend to have a family discussion. I prayed to God to help me deliver this news without breaking down in front of my family. I didn't want to appear defeated, but on the inside, I was shattered by the news. It was growing more real to me day by day. My oldest, Shalyn, sat on the sofa and begin to wail as I made my announcement, my youngest, Kristyn, gave a blank stare, my husband, Lionel, emotionless, trying to hold it together. My daughters had recently come to Dallas for a visit in September so we could have mother and daughter time and celebrate their birthdays. Now I am sitting in the den delivering news that could ultimately change our family dynamics forever.

And I couldn't make a promise that I didn't know if I would be able to keep. The reality is, I could die. But I may live too. I choose Life. Later that day, I called my mother and sister, Natalie with the news. Natalie would come to Dallas to be with me for the MRI appointment. We didn't dwell on the diagnosis when she arrived. We focused on enjoying our sister time together, shopping, and dining at some of our favorite places. I didn't immediately tell my extended family; it took about a week for me to gather my thoughts and figure out how I wanted to let them know. I sent a group text. I couldn't make separate phone calls giving the same message and answering the same questions. One of my texts begin like this:

Hey Family, just wanted to update you'll on my cancer journey...

Even though I have been open about past ailments, the breast cancer diagnosis would bring out a vulnerable side in me that I wasn't sure I could handle. Questions that I couldn't answer. For example, I didn't have any signs or symptoms that would have alerted me to think that I would have a breast cancer diagnosis. I had had an infected hair follicle under my left arm that ended up needing to be lanced weeks prior to the diagnosis, but cancerous tumors were found in the right breast. I didn't know how to explain this to myself or anyone else. I had no clues. I knew that my mammogram the year prior showed no abnormalities. I performed self-breast examinations monthly, sometimes more. I didn't feel any lumps in either breast.

This path was yet to be taken, a journey into unknown territory and the control factor in me, that's feels safe following the steps; didn't have the blueprint to follow. A cancer diagnosis can catch you off guard taking you to a lonely space.

I sent separate messages with the same content to my three besties.

The news produced an immediate reactive phone call with speechless conversation. I just held on to the phone.

After receiving the news, my bestie Katina in Texas brought one of her friends, who I'll call Survivor M, over to my apartment who had gone through the process and was a 10-year breast cancer survivor. She appeared physically fit, open to conversation, and upbeat in spirit. Survivor M encouraged me, she looked well. We sat on the sofa in my apartment and talked for a couple of hours. I had many questions. How painful was the breast mastectomy surgery? How many drains I would have? How do I not pull the drains out by mistake? How long it would take to lift my arms again? What did she do to help herself? Did she have stitches? Did having to stretch the chest muscle for implants hurt? Did she have sensation in her breasts? Did she still have her own nipples? How did her breasts feel with implants and had she had any complications with the implants?

Yes, these were questions that I needed to ask the doctor, and I did eventually. But there was nothing like having a person who had walked in these shoes answer these pertinent questions for me in that moment. Survivor M had chosen to have a bilateral mastectomy and reconstruction with breast implants. She gave me details about her procedure, and she defended her decisions and treatment options. I asked her if she would show me what her breast implants looked like, and she gladly gave me a full view. At the end of our encounter, we exchanged phone numbers, and Survivor M told me to call her whenever I needed to.

After all conversations with my family and friends, I began to start the process of understanding my diagnosis, still anxious but hopeful. My takeaway from all the conversations had me thinking about my options. For example, I was unsure about wanting implants. I wasn't sure about foreign elements being introduced into my body; my gut told me 'No', the implants felt different to me. Survivor M's were beautifully reconstructed. The implants were perky, no bra required, the areolas had been tattooed to a real-like appearance, but she had impaired sensation. I reminisced on the time I had desired to have a "boob" job and a tummy tuck for cosmetic purposes, which a lot of women desire, especially after having children. Now, the idea was unwanted, even sickening to me.

I wanted this diagnosis to go away. I reached out to my diagnosed sorority sisters and solicited their experiences. I needed to hear about their journeys.

My initial oncologist, Dr. Kory Jones, at USMD hospital in Arlington, Texas, was wonderful. She took the time with me to explain everything from a diagnostic standpoint. She referred me to a plastic surgeon, who was also great, and provided me with the latest surgical procedures available. He marked, measured, and photographed me, because I was uncertain of where I would have my surgery performed. Interestingly, after taking the Breast Cancer Gene test (BRCA) to determine my risks or connect the dots with my mom having breast cancer prior, my test resulted in uncertainty, a non-variant status. Now, I am really puzzled, what is the source of this breast cancer diagnosis?

I vacillated between having the surgery performed in Texas or Mississippi. I didn't want to give up the trainee position or lose momentum. After weighing my options, getting approved for telework and considering my support systems, I made the choice to return home to Mississippi. I got connected with one of the best oncologists in my area, Dr. Guangzhi Qu. He was a praying doctor. He would oversee my treatment plan after the initial surgery at St. Charles Surgical Hospital in New Orleans. And I tried not to think of my job, or the feeling of not completing what I was chosen to do. I had to focus on my health, my well-being, and what I needed to do and needed to know moving forward in the breast cancer journey, step by step.

When I prepared to leave Texas, I didn't have adequate sick leave and vacation to cover a long period of time off. I had no idea of what amount of time I needed to recover, or if recovery would be my story. I filed for FMLA to protect my job. The employees in Texas showed overwhelming support. Many people, including those I didn't know, donated sick leave, which carried me through with a paycheck for almost four months. I wondered how long I would be off my feet, and how long would I need to be still to heal properly.

In the midst of my storm, my husband had a car accident. The car accident was the thunder in my storm. My husband would need surgery on his shoulder, but my surgery would come first. The thunder in my storm turned into a blessing, as I had my husband at home with me to tend to my care at every phase of my journey. Many of my supporters had to remain at a distance due to the pandemic, so at a time when I desired to have people rallied around me, the uncertainty of the pandemic kept everyone away. I couldn't afford to risk my health with a compromised immune system and open wounds. The feelings of loneliness entered even when my immediate family was right beside me every step of the way. There were some days darkness set in, a depressive spirit. The most memorable days were after my first chemotherapy treatment. The first day of treatment was overwhelming. I didn't know what to expect. I was told to be prepared to remain at the appointment for three hours. This would be the longest appointment due to all the paperwork, education on the drug therapy, monitoring, etc. I knew other people's stories, but I couldn't picture mine.

Honestly, I didn't want to be here. I had chemotherapy in the same building where my oncologist's office is located. I sat in the same waiting area only to enter a different section of the floor. When they called my name, I cringed thinking to myself, "Dammit, here I go." It was the longest thirty feet I had ever walked. The chemotherapy area had an open section with multiple reclining chairs with televisions hanging from the ceiling, a few privacy curtains, and private rooms. For my first treatment, I requested a private room, and the office accommodated me. I desired a private room because I didn't want people staring at me or asking questions. I had no desire to talk about the breast cancer. I wanted to concentrate on me. I had so many thoughts running through my mind. I thought I would become sick as soon as the chemotherapy entered my body. I was very emotional, and anxious.

To my surprise, the rooms were filled with people of all ages. It shocked me to see so many affected by the same fate. Most people appeared with solemn faces, a few were talkative, some sleeping. I entered the area in a state of shock. My body was numb, but my heart thumped in my chest. I felt anxious, and I wanted to vomit. I was glad that I wasn't alone, my husband accompanied me to every treatment. So, do you really want to know what receiving chemotherapy feels like?

Chemotherapy is a beastly experience in my opinion. I had surgery a week prior for placement of a port-a-catheter in my chest to administer the chemotherapy medications. The port-a-catheter placement remained sore and swollen. I was prescribed pain numbing cream to use before receiving chemotherapy. The medications consisted of a cocktail to kill the cancerous cells and to help with the possible nausea and itching that could flare. I felt a burning sensation all over my body as these chemicals entered my body. I got hot, then cold and sleepy. The medications are administered slowly and steadily. I remained in the same room for three hours lying in a recliner watching television and sometimes, it watched me. The administering nurse checked on me regularly to make sure I was tolerating the treatment without reaction. I closed my eyes and tried to sleep. I imagined what my next hours would feel like, what my next days would bring. I imagined this being over and done. After the first treatment, I felt rejuvenated. I had energy after leaving the office, and I went home and resumed my routine. I didn't do much because I was healing from the surgery, so I watched television, read some inspirational quotes, and sat outside on the patio furniture just to get some fresh air for a while.

On Day Two, though, my body began to slow down, uncontrolled by me. I moved slower. I couldn't think or comprehend quickly. It took more time to remember my own name. By Day Three, I couldn't move and I felt fatigued. Everything appeared to be moving in slow motion. How could this cocktail of drugs take away my pep? I lay in bed not wanting to eat. I didn't take a bath. I hardly moved; only my eyes as I gazed at television. It felt like the worst hangover ever. And it had been a long time since I had been inebriated. (Good thing, I don't drink like that anymore!) Lying there in my bed, I remained calm. This was a new place for me, not being able to get up and bathe myself, not wanting to eat. I drifted in and out of sleep.

My mother would call daily, and I was too tired to hold the phone, so I hit the speaker button and just listened. She encouraged me to just take a bite of something if only a saltine cracker. I told her I would, but I just wanted to sleep. Everything in my body slowed, even my breathing. I couldn't inhale deeply; the beast had taken control. Day Four was another day of stillness, but I managed to sponge off with some assistance. Then, back to bed. I forced some soup in my mouth; I swallowed only two sips of the soup, but the broth, tasted weird. The metallic taste buds were in high gear, no more soup or anything for me today, I'll pass.

By Day 5, I was more conscious, more awake. I moved to the den and sat in the power lift recliner that I had acquired after my dad's passing. The recliner had remained in the garage for months now, here it was I needed it and all the functions it offered. I remembered how my dad looked sitting in his chair, he liked the functions of the power lift chair that almost stood him in an erect position, but he forgot that he could no longer walk without assistance. Sitting in his chair frightened me, would this treatment plan to defeat breast cancer take away my independence? I required a second surgery only three weeks after the first because cancer was also found in my lymph nodes. More lymph nodes had to be removed and tested. Prior to the first chemotherapy treatment, I lay in that chair for one month, sleeping and eating.

The bed in my bedroom was too high for me to climb into so I opted for the power recliner, I made it cozy, piling on multiple blankets, my soft pillow, wearing my fuzzy socks and beanie cap although I still had hair on my head before the first chemotherapy treatment. Chemotherapy had my body experiencing hot and cold spells on top of the hot flashes that had recently begun prior to the diagnosis. Here I was, partially confined to this recliner in the den, from day to night. When everyone went to their respective bedrooms, I would lie awake, restlessly, at night in the chair, staring at the transom over the back door. Looking at the night sky, my mind drifted, sometimes wondering if death would be my fate. Sometimes, I cried myself to sleep because this was the only time, I would allow myself to feel weak when no one was watching. I couldn't allow my family to see me appearing to give up. I couldn't give up. One week after having chemo, my body had adjusted, some of my strength returned, and I moved around the house being cautious not to snag my drains on anything. Just walking on the first floor of my home exhausted my energy resources, so going upstairs was not an option. I was thankful for having a bedroom with a full bathroom downstairs even if I couldn't sleep in the bed. What they don't tell you about chemotherapy treatments is that it knocks you off your feet, but as soon as you find your bearings and begin to get back up, it's time for the next treatment-----Damn!

And the cycle continues until it's your turn to ring the bell.

Good People Don't Deserve Cancer

R eflecting on my life, I've always wanted to be a good child. The child who caused no trouble, who wouldn't get a bad report from my teachers. I wanted to shine and it was expected. I've always considered myself to be loyal to a fault. I'm the friend who follows the loyalty code, and the one who wouldn't crack under pressure. I'm the person who has and continues to hold shared secrets without speaking of or on those secrets unless the person who has entrusted me to secrecy revisits the conversation. I feel like loyalty should be rewarded.

Being good to people should not end up with a diagnosis of breast cancer. Where is this coming from? What did I do to deserve this? Having cancer sucks. Now here is one more thing to add to this life so full of ups and downs, one more obstacle to overcome. I have wondered "why me" as I've tried to be a good person. Why do I deserve to have breast cancer? I've given my all to my family; my daughters are now young adults and in college. And here comes this doggone breast cancer out of nowhere. When I initially received the diagnosis, my emotions became unpredictable. In one minute, I was in shock. In the next moment, I was crying. Then, I became angry. The anger came from inside bursting with emotions and bewildered by the thought that my genuine nature of being giving, caring, and trying to be a good person would render such a fate. I have sacrificed many things to make sure others had what they needed. I have given so much of me that I've gotten lost trying to do good deeds. I am the epitome of an imperfect perfection, and my mold is irreplaceable.

Breast cancer was the disease that entered my life, altering my plans. Stopping my moment to reach my goals. The one moment I, once again, had a chance to shine, to become the difference, could be gone because I needed to stop and take care of this health problem. Truth be told, I just wanted some peace, with no health issues, not having to take care of anyone else. Before being diagnosed with breast cancer, I felt good, and I looked good. I was exercising, I was working to become an overall better version of myself.

Being a good person takes work. I have been consistent in my faith, consistent in being a wife and mother, consistent in being a good daughter, sister, and friend, consistent in my work ethic, consistent in treating others well even when not reciprocated. Good people don't deserve cancer, right?

What I do know is that cancer of any nature does not discriminate. It will and can attack the good, the bad, the best and the worst person. It has no filter on any race. I had a hard time adjusting to the fact that all my efforts of consciously trying to live as a solidly good human being, breast cancer would be my nemesis. All I could reflect on is the passage in the Bible, John 10:10-11 KJV, that states, "***The thief cometh not, but for to steal, and to*** *kill, and to destroy: I am come that they might have life, and they might have it more abundantly. I am the good shepherd: the good shepherd giveth his life for the sheep. "*

The breast cancer diagnosis felt like a hard blow to my abdomen. Good people shouldn't have to suffer at this level. As I began to ingest the diagnosis, I realized that being considered any type of person, good, bad or indifferent, never mattered. This was my walk, my journey. **CANCER** is *Cancer* is cancer.

I have changed my perspective view from questioning, "Why this would happen to a good person like me?" to "Why not a good person like me?" The justification is a good person like me now has a testimony. A good person like me is cancer free and a survivor. I once heard a pastor preach, "It's not about the storm, but how you come through it, what will you look like after its gone. So, how do I look now? I'm changed from the inside to the outside. Am I still a good person? I consider myself to be. And the point I really want to make is having breast cancer didn't change that part of me. Breast cancer didn't make me bitter. I didn't hold on to the initial anger despite the rollercoaster of emotions-- depression, some anxiety. I've had human moments. But I also have a spiritual foundation, a team of praying family, friends, church members, sorority sisters, people unknown to me sending positive inspiration for a full recovery.

This chapter of my book keeps me laughing every time I read it. Good people don't deserve cancer----who determines the good people? I now realize how judgmental this title may seem, but it's my truth, what I thought and felt going through my journey, my storm. Do not think about who, what, or why if you should face a diagnosis of cancer. Think about, "Why not me?" Look at the fate with this attitude, "Hmm-Cancer chose the right person now, baby!" And give yourself room to understand that cancer doesn't discriminate. You didn't do anything wrong. Just like some people win the lottery, some people get cancer. Some people win the lottery and get cancer. Do you get where I'm going with this? Embrace all things happening in your life and make the most of it. This self-proclaimed, "Good person" is proof that lemons turn into lemonade when you add the right amount of sugar to suit your taste. It's all about the way you perceive the obstacles in your life. I chose to stay positive, stay sweetened, drank my lemonade and weather the storm. Everyone has obstacles just keep living.

Just Cry

I'm afraid to cry. I am stuck wondering if I let the river of tears flow will it keep the cancer away. Will it free me of the anxiety and pain that I've had to face since the surgeries and chemotherapy? My life is different now. At times, I feel like I'm outside of my body looking in. When I do cry, it's not from a thought or emotion; the tears just begin to flow out of nowhere, a silent cry. I can be driving, walking, or sleeping, and a stream of salty water begins flowing down my face. The tears seem trapped inside of me from a place that I can't open automatically. It's strange to me because, though the incisions have healed externally, I haven't. I've got an ocean within me with riptides that can take me so fast that I've had to pull over on the road while driving because the stream wouldn't stop flowing for me to drive safely. These tears appear when I'm by myself when I feel alone.

In the presence of others, I wear a stoic face. I appear to be okay. I hold these tears, and I don't know why. The internal tears seem to keep me attached to the cancer. I'm still in disbelief some days that this has happened to me. Some days, I think I'm dreaming, then I cry. I cry in the shower where I can be alone. I cry an ugly cry, snot dripping, lips shivering, but not loud. I ask God to protect me. I don't know why I hold on to the tears. Maybe I do it so I won't be able to forget the pain and processes that I've endured. I feel bound by the tears. But when I do cry, the stream flows and flows and flows. I feel sad, I feel anxious, I feel mad as hell sometimes, I ache on the inside wondering why I have always had to pay the price and carry the overwhelming load. As I am writing this, the tears are flowing. All forms of cancer suck.

I hope that as I release the pressure, telling my story, that I just cry and if you find yourself in the same situation, you'll just cry too.

The Release

The release. I dealt with a lot of life events from my teenage years through my adulthood. I have always felt strong enough to handle the situations that presented themselves. And I usually defeated those experiences with certainty. But this breast cancer diagnosis took my breath away. It put a lump in my throat. it made me nauseous. It stabbed me in the gut with a twist to the knife. I found myself experiencing the pain of whatever I had tucked away or felt that I had defeated re-surfacing. Having breast cancer and having to be vulnerable enough to allow other people to help me, was a place that I was unfamiliar with. Having breast cancer forced me to let go of locked away stressors I hadn't really let go of, even though I thought I had. For example, I had to let go of my desire to be the person always to the rescue. I needed help. I needed to be rescued. I had hidden my feelings for so long, and my lack of emotions appeared stronger than I was. I wasn't strong at all.

The uncertainty of the breast cancer diagnosis and outcome showed me that this was something more grandiose than I ever imagined. What have I learned? I have learned to release the small stuff and some of the big stuff too, I learned to accept. I learned to free myself from others' problems. I had to control what I let people give to me in spirit and in communication. I declined to offer advice. I decided not to be the problem solver.

A different person returned home after the first surgery, not just from a surgical standpoint, but also from the realization that if I could withstand surgery and trust a team of surgeons for twelve hours to put me back together and make me whole again, then why in the hell am I holding on to all the life events that I had overcome. Why was I tucking all these emotions away? Why did I feel the need to carry all these life obstacles or burdens with me for the rest of my life? Even though I consider myself to have a great life, having many of the luxuries that some people would consider accomplished, I was boxed in. I let everyday life experiences place a silence in my heart that I carried around on my best days and my worst. Having to face breast cancer awakened me to a place that I had to listen. I didn't have the masterplan. I didn't have the right song. I didn't have anything to fix the problem, and I didn't have any room left to hide my emotions. I had to let it all go. I had to reexamine my life, refocus, and release.

I found that having to remain still allowed me to really hear my thoughts, to hear others, to accept everyday life with more gratitude. I could only walk a short distance after my surgery, so I would go to the back porch and open the door to get some fresh air and listen to the birds chirping or a car passing by. I found my still time to add patience in my life. And with every breath I took after the first surgery, I let go of a negative feeling or thought that I had carried with me for so long.

The diagnosis of breast cancer lifted burdens unseen and unspoken. Instantly, I began to inhale deep, deep, and deeper. The fresh air flowing in from the back door being inhaled was exhaled with pollution. Standing in the doorway of my home with my breast tissue gone, my abdomen cut open, made me realize that life was short lived, and I had the responsibility to live better, I owed this to myself. I could feel the healing begin.

Why hadn't I allowed this to happen sooner? I really didn't know. All this time, I considered myself to be a person of great faith and through all the biblical teachings I knew, I was faltering. It took something of this magnitude to get my attention.

I experienced a life-threatening situation in 2017, I had a surgical procedure, and one of the medications I was prescribed caused a gastric ulcer to form in my stomach. I came very near death by the time I realized I was bleeding internally. I had to receive six pints of blood, but the outcomes didn't alter my body externally. Now, I was facing what many women with breast cancer go through. How am I going to look after this surgery? Will I be botched? You never go to the place of asking yourself, will I look better, will I be better?

The vanity of wanting to look and be at our best takes a toll on the healthiest, wealthiest, sickest, and the poorest. I had to remind myself that beauty on the outside is only skin deep, but to have an inner beauty that radiates for all to see is TRUE beauty and no amount of makeup nor skincare line could produce that look. Allowing myself to not take on other people's burdens, letting go of other people's dung, and accepting God's will in life and death allowed me to release myself of self-criticism. I realized I was, and will always be, an imperfect perfection freed me of many strongholds. And it was only when I was freed with the acceptance of having flaws that could be seen, I was able to release the binding burdens.

The inner healing has slowly given me life again in a place that is far and unknown. Writing this book and facing my feelings is reflective of and elevating to my soul. I really hope someone out there with health issues can relate. I hope the process of learning to release binding burdens reaches all people before they are affected by an awakening moment. A piercing moment for me was accepting, processing, and going through the physical, the emotional, the spiritual, the awakening of past burdens that pivoted the old me into the new me. And for all these growing moments, for all the elevation, I'm forever grateful. I am indebted to remain. I like this place of serenity. I like being able to say, "I can't. I'm not. I won't…" Prior to having breast cancer, I allowed myself to be stretched so thin as if I were superwoman. Now, I had no other options. I wasn't physically or mentally in shape to run to anyone's rescue, not even my own. I felt less pressure to be everyone's everything. On this day, I am Nicole. I am Nicole who is recovering from having breast cancer, and yes, she is selfish with herself. I am letting go. I'm not overthinking. I'm not trying to fix it. I am going with the flow of things today, tomorrow, next week and so on. I like this space it feels good to just do Me.

Happy Feelings

H appiness is a choice and having breast cancer can make you feel as if you are being robbed of that choice. When going through any life-altering journey, remember the happier times. Make more happy times. I am happy when I am with my family. I'm happy around my closest friends. I like time alone to think, meditate, and read. I am happy when I help other people; it makes my heart skip a beat to see a smile on someone's face. I am happy when I can contribute to others' happiness. I am happy when I splurge on myself though not always a big splurge; any self-care and retail therapy work for me. I'm happy when I go on vacation. I like white sandy beaches, blue waters, good vibes. I can lay on the beach for hours listening to the ocean waves crash while reading a book sipping on a refreshment. I'm happy on holidays, because it involves my entire family. I'm happy on my birthday, because I know I made another solar return, and I don't take it for granted. Never have. Never will. My happiest times are with the people I enjoy and love. I've lost many family members and friends, but the memories allow me to feel happy. Happy to have shared my life with the people I love. My hope is if you are faced with this journey that you will find that place, that spot, that comfort zone where happiness trickles in, where your mind rejects any negative thoughts and produce HAPPY FEELINGS.

Help And Hope

✦

Romans 12:12 (KJV)

Rejoicing in hope; patient in tribulation; continuing instant
in prayer.

The pink ribbon of "hope" has been a symbol in the fight for anyone diagnosed with breast cancer. I wrote a Breast cancer speech centered on the idea of having "Hope." The organizer of the Breast Cancer Awareness/ Domestic Violence event at my job asked me to speak after I revealed that I was a survivor. Honestly, this was one of the few times that I had given any thought of myself being a "survivor." My message detailed my journey of the events that led to the diagnosis, my feelings of being hopeless, my reflection of those scriptures I leaned on to when my days appeared darker and the driving spirit within me, my "flight or fight" response never allowed me to give up.

When I wrote this speech, I wanted to touch someone who had experienced, witnessed, or was currently on the journey. My speech produced a rippling effect of emotions throughout the gathered crowd. I received accolades from many in the emotional expression of females and males who weren't afraid to share with me their personal experiences with breast cancer.

As I delivered my speech, tears began to stream down my make-up beaten face. As I closed, my emotions were clearly visible to the audience. I allowed my mask of strength to come off in front of complete strangers, some family, and friends. At the end of my speech, I shared a collage of pictures that I put together through every phase of my journey. I wanted to show what hopelessness turned into hope looked like. I had taken these pictures throughout my surgical procedures, on some of my most challenging days, feeling hopeless, and on some of my better days, feeling hopeful.

HELP

About nine months after my initial surgery to remove the cancerous tumors from my right breast, I participated in the University of Alabama at Birmingham Breast Cancer Recovery Study. At this point of my journey, I needed to talk to someone to express my true feelings and gain insight into how to regain my life and lifestyle. I was assigned a licensed occupational therapist named Jennifer. The study was compensated for four sessions, soliciting my feedback on a pool of topics. These sessions were over the phone and lasted between thirty minutes to an hour. Jennifer was always upbeat, rarely called late, and if there was a contact issue, it was acknowledged timely and rescheduled to meet my needs as soon as possible. We discussed everyday activities and various topics; yet, when she asked questions about my feelings, I felt targeted and exposed. I looked in the mirror and saw all the reflection of a new self, the person that I hadn't really introduced myself to.

Breast cancer and the treatments had changed me inside and out. I felt like I was in a canal floating along without knowing my name, unidentified. All I knew at this point was I had breast cancer, had the cancerous breasts tissue removed, received chemotherapy, and everything in my life had changed.

Jennifer was good at her job, she kept me focused on the positive. In every session, she reminded me that I was still valuable and needed in my family. And the reason why I had agreed to participate in this study was to help those who were on a similar path. I had mixed emotions with every conversation with Jennifer. On some of the calls, I was a fighting warrior ready to battle until the end. Other calls, I was emotional, crying from just answering the phone, silent without words, listening, in pain, in fear, afraid. I was depressed. Sometimes, I just wanted to hear her discuss things not about breast cancer, like how her children were doing and what were her plans for the weekend with her family. And, luckily, as we built a comfortable space with each other, she would share some of her life, and I loved hearing about it. Jennifer's openness made me remember how life is constant, moving at a far greater pace than any of us realize until you are faced with a challenge that makes you look in the mirror and really see. I needed to stop being reminded that the only reason she was calling was to discuss the aftermath of my breast cancer situation and all that follows. I wanted to feel like nothing had happened, like my normal was still the same, my mirror image hadn't changed.

HOPE

There have been very few times in my life that I can remember the feelings of being hopeless. Receiving and experiencing the diagnosis of having breast cancer has gained one of these spots. I felt all alone, even though I knew several people who had gone through this journey. Yes, I found myself in an internalized hopeless stupor for months. I didn't want my family to see me as weak, so I showed no signs of hopelessness. I kept the emotion bottled up inside corked and capped. I felt that if I showed myself hopeless, my daughters wouldn't be able to watch me in such a weakened state. I wanted to appear strong for them. I didn't want my family to absorb my pain. I didn't want them to know I was in pain. I was in pain emotionally and physically. I wanted to appear strong and try to maintain as normal a lifestyle as I could while going on this journey.

In the process of writing this book, I decided to ask my daughters, two pertinent questions:

1. How did you feel when I told you I had breast cancer?
2. How did it feel when you had to help take care of me?

Shalyn stated,

"I felt like I was going to lose you, and everything froze because I didn't want to accept the fact that this was real. Taking care of you was by far the hardest thing I've had to do because I've never wanted to see you down. I was trying my hardest to be strong and stay in a positive mindset for the both of us, but there were many nights and moments now when I think about that time, and I cry."

Kristyn stated,

"Hearing the initial news that you were diagnosed with breast cancer caused my mind to think the worst. I immediately thought that God was preparing us for a life without you being here since you had temporarily moved to Dallas for a new job position. We were already having to experience not having you readily available. Since I was away at college, I didn't experience the day-to-day care you needed. The time I spent away at school was an escape from the reality of you being at home and sick. The times I was present, I didn't like to see you, nor did I want to accept that you were sick. It was hard to watch and even harder to help knowing my help couldn't change the diagnosis."

Whew!

I wasn't surprised by their answers, but until now I had never inquired or spoken on the subject, because I wasn't ready to receive these answers. Silently, my heart ached every time I needed to have my daughters help me. It's not supposed to be this way, not at this age. I am supposed to be helping them. I recall that day; I was sitting in the wheelchair, and I needed assistance taking steps to the toilet. I was too weak to lift myself up or pivot to sit down. This was the moment I silently cried when they closed the door to the bathroom, and I sat their weeping in pain and feeling like the end could be near. My independence was gone.

As a mother, I've wanted to protect my children from any pain, but the truth is, I was on an uncertain path and unpredictable outcome, and I couldn't promise great results. I remained conscious in the moments and tackled the inevitable events day by day.

Set Back Up

I had a few setbacks during this journey. None that could be forecast. I previously mentioned my surgical procedure to receive a port-a-catheter for chemotherapy treatments. The catheter was placed on the left side of my chest below the clavicle bone, better known as the collarbone, on February 3. The catheter placement produced pain and swelling that never ceased. I received my first chemotherapy treatment nine days after placement on February 12.

On February 27, my birthday, I was rushed to the hospital. Five days prior on a Monday, I had begun having chills and shaking uncontrollably. I thought it was part of the process. I called and went to my doctor's office on Wednesday, complaining of bone pain with a low-grade fever. I was prescribed some pain medication to alternate with Tylenol, a fever reducer. By Friday, I couldn't walk and was confined to a wheelchair, needing assistance to stand and walk four feet to use the commode. I was sick. I was seeing double, but I didn't tell anyone. I thought it was the result of taking pain medication. In hindsight, I should have made my oncologist' staff and my family aware of the state I was in. My body was sending warning signals that something in my body was not functioning correctly, but I was attempting to appear strong on my birthday, my special day. My daughters got me up, helped me shower, and get dressed. They were in on the surprise. I was greeted by some of my closest friends via zoom. Having some of my closest friends remember me on my special day was awesome. I felt loved. They took turns talking, laughing, and reminiscing. I only offered up minimum gestures of conversation. I was extremely weak and exhausted. My day was planned to be filled with my immediate family coming over with a special dinner to be with me, but it never happened.

By 4:00 p.m., I was headed full speed to the emergency room at St. Dominic hospital with a fever of 105 degrees, shaking uncontrollably, draped in a thick blanket, unable to urinate, frightened. I knew I was dying. I began to have blackouts in the car. "Lord, please don't let me die" was all I kept thinking. The diagnosis, this time, was sepsis. I was in a bad state. I remained in the hospital for ten days; for five of those days I was unable to walk. I remember lying in the hospital bed wanting to get up, but I was too weak. My husband called on our pastor, Pastor LeYonn Armstrong, to tell him of my illness. Visitor restrictions remained during this time, but my pastor was allowed. He touched my feet and he prayed. His prayer was biblical and comforted my soul. He prayed a prayer of complete healing and told me I would walk out of the hospital. "Yes, I am going to walk again," I spoke over myself. After several days receiving strong antibiotics and seeing numerous physicians, I was able to leave the hospital. I was wheeled down in a wheelchair to the patient pick-up area. I asked the transporter to stop at the entryway. He asked if I was sure, I said "yes," I got up from the wheelchair stood slightly bent over, and I walked to the car. I was determined not to be in anyone's wheelchair anytime soon. Let's go home! I remained on intravenous antibiotics at home under the care of a home health nurse for another month, then back to chemotherapy.

Other setbacks included an infection on the back of my head that landed me back in the emergency room to be lanced, needing more antibiotics. After the first surgery, my left breast had a small triangular area that needed more attending to with Tegaderm dressings and Hydrophilic cream. This was a slow process monitored weekly by my surgeon's team. My white blood cells bottomed out while receiving chemotherapy, causing the need to return one day after chemotherapy to receive a Neupogen injection to boost the production of white blood cells. White blood cells help fight off infections in your body. The injection caused bone pain. I even needed an iron infusion at the end of the chemotherapy treatments. And let me address the metallic taste and nausea. Yes, I experienced both of these things. Another cancer surviving friend, Julia, told me about drinking pickle juice to relieve the nausea and it worked for me. My appetite increased and the metallic taste diminished.

All these setbacks set me back up. Every time I thought about giving up something deep inside said, "Nope, not gonna happen." I've had a total of six surgeries in a 9-month span, five surgeries requiring anesthesia. And I am still here, living and breathing amid a viral pandemic.

Don't Waste Your Cancer

The horrifying six letter word, **C-A-N-C-E-R**, leads most to believe that there is no hope, that life ends the moment the doctor enters the room and gives you the diagnosis. Well, I'm here to tell you it doesn't. Don't waste your cancer. Don't waste your time waiting to die or thinking you're going to die. After the initial shock, make every day a day cancer must fight to get your attention. The way we look at the outcome may not be a perfect picture with a fairy tale ending but it's still your life, your journey, your story.

My journey with breast cancer has been one of the most breathtaking situations I've encountered in my life. Yet, here I am cancer free, minimum stress, and more equipped to face my life head on. I feel free from the stigmatism that most face when given a possible terminal diagnosis, "I'm just waiting to die." I'm not waiting to die. I'm living. And it took being diagnosed with breast cancer to make life easier. I no longer worry about the outcomes. I prepare every day for the victory. I could be weighed down, broken by the experience, but what good would that produce. Part of this journey was met with attitude and hope. The attitude that cancer was not going to win. Remember, I thought good people shouldn't get cancer. I'm still laughing, I'm still smiling. As I searched through my personal photographs of every moment I could capture on this journey, I noticed a consistent and constant expression. In 99% of these visibly transforming photographs, I'm smiling. I found a way to muster away the tears for a smile. I knew one day I would look back at these moments and wonder how I got to this point; how I made it through. The simplest answer is, I didn't waste my cancer.

I have used this journey to learn more about myself than I ever knew. I've allowed my vulnerability to show and open my heart, except all flaws, become more patient, take time to just be still and to be okay with the good days along with the not so good days. After treatment, I'm still in recovery. It takes time to heal emotionally and physically. I have days where fatigue sets in, and I sit down to take my rest. I have days I feel I'm at my best. I use the best days and make them count. I no longer put off doing what I want to do if my energy level allows. I live, take my medications, and I don't wait for cancer. I don't wait in fear that cancer will resurface. The idea has crept into my mind a few times, but I immediately say, "Go away." I don't want any of my time to be wasted on cancer. I am cancer free today. I am healthy. I look forward to life and the moments. Making the most of these moments is what is important to me. Memories will last a lifetime, and I intend to leave many memories for my family, friends, and anyone whose path I may cross. I'm going to share this journey, share this experience. Don't allow having cancer or having had cancer to regulate your life. Don't waste it.

I am more intentional, more determined, more intrigued by the life I have been afforded. I wouldn't change my journey. The shoes I walk in were definitively only made for me. I don't want to waste my cancer journey. I want the world to know that although every outcome does not guarantee life, cancer should not be the focus. Focus on living. Focus on letting go of any hiccups or hang ups that have caused stress. When you identify your weaknesses, be vulnerable enough to let others see them, accept help, and be free. Be positive in this journey even on the days that zap your strength. Remember that you never walk alone, even when it gets lonely. Embrace the pain, be still and listen. Listen to hear the inner voice that helps keep you sane. Take time to take a deep breath and look in the mirror. Don't waste your cancer. Let it go!

Then Breathe.

Epiphany

I wrote this book on my journey of having breast cancer, because I want people to free themselves of the stressors of life before they become sickened. I want to show how the diagnosis of having breast cancer, going through all the surgeries, chemotherapy treatments, and some setbacks didn't stop my desire and hope for progress and life. I want people to understand the process. Having breast cancer was a life changing experience that has changed me in many ways, but also has brought me to a place in my life where I had to release some real stuff, stressors that had me bound. I want people to know that breast cancer affects men and women. There is a greater need to have routine check-ups.

Go see the doctor.

Having breast cancer gave me back my life in a new way. I'm in a new season and flawed with good intentions. I had to let go of the impatient me, realizing that at my lowest moments, patience was all I could cling too. I had to be open to being more vulnerable, learning to accept help with open arms. The breast cancer diagnosis wasn't what scared me the most. I had to come to terms with my most inner insecurities. I was uncomfortable with not being everyone's saving grace, because now I needed people. I was afraid of losing my independence. I am accustomed to being the "Go to person" and not being able to help myself or anyone else frightened me. I could not imagine relinquishing my role as a giver and becoming needy.

I needed people, known and unknown. I needed the phone calls, the zoom chats, the spiritual literature that arrived in the mail, the food being delivered, the thoughtfulness, the care packages, the concern from others. I needed to know people were cheering me on from a distance to be well again. I had to graciously accept the diagnosis, the surgical procedures, the chemotherapy, the infected port-a- catheter that placed me in the hospital for ten days with sepsis. I experienced a loss of my independent nature, and this really scared the heck out of me. From walking into the hospital and walking out to being bound to a wheelchair less than two months after. (Mind you, this is the same the wheelchair that I saw my dad never get up from after having multiple strokes along with other ailments.) When I had to sit in that wheelchair all I could think about is how my father must have felt so helpless. Because this is how it felt to me, I was helpless and so fatigued. Sitting in the wheelchair depressed me. The thought of not walking again made me want to give up. It was at the time when I couldn't manage to stand up after being pushed to the toilet. My daughters assisted and helped me take the four steps to sit on the toilet, then I needed help to get back up. Not being able to help myself almost made me lose my mind. I couldn't fathom the idea of being in this state continuously. My mind could only think of all the good things I had accomplished and how I was not nearly finished, but what if I never walked again? I was not going to be okay with the idea of having to be dependent and at the mercies of everyone else, at least that's how I felt in my mind. There's a saying that goes, "If you want to make God laugh, tell him your plans." I have planned, produced, starred in, and created my own comedy show in my mind and the laughs have landed at great costs, yet God has remained constant in my life.

I realize that I am driven with a sense to aspire, achieve, and accomplish. And I have been equipped with the knowledge, the independence, the resources, the will to overcome. I now laugh at the idea that being considered a good person would keep cancer away from me. I'm still laughing at this thought. I had to learn to be more patient in my walks and thoughts, to be more vulnerable and open to needing to need people. To allow others in and let go of the controllable and uncontrollable situations, to be more accepting. Breast cancer freed me. I had to be moved by something that was so unpredictable to free myself from the past, live in the present, and push forward to the future. What I have accepted is I am walking in my truth; I have empathy for all diagnosed with any form of cancer. I am a breast cancer survivor, thriver, and witness to a life experience that many have succumb to. I do think about the what ifs from time to time. What if cancer decides to invade my life again?

I didn't have the expectation of my breast cancer walk, or that my journey was different from anyone else's, but I do know the shoes I walk in were made just for me. And it's a snug fit. Don't let the small problems grow. Make adjustments in your life often to suit your moments without apology. Live healthier by making modifications in your life. My modifications began with changing my food choices and getting back into the routine of working out at home and in the gym to release stress. Turn the music up loud and dance. Live a life unafraid to receive help especially when you are most in need. Live a life that is intentional, allowing for failures to happen, allowing for imperfections, and allow God to be your guide.

I encourage anyone reading this book to not be afraid of breast cancer or any other diagnosed ailments that may arise in your life. Take a look in the mirror and don't be afraid to see the new you. Make it your journey and continue to live your life. Let people in your life know your heart. Let those that care help you along the way. Remain hopeful and your days ahead will not be filled with hopelessness. Enjoy the moments and make memories. And when you need to cry, let it all out, scream if you need to, let the snot drool down your face, but after this moment make sure you find something to smile about too. Allow happy feelings to remind you that cancer is not a sentence of life or death. May your days be filled with intentional purpose.

Don't waste your cancer on yourself. Don't be selfish. Share the experience with others; you'll be surprised by the lives you will touch. Realize that if you don't give your testimony no one will ever know. Why won't they know? Because if you don't waste your cancer, you will never show signs of the illness. Even with the loss of hair, your beauty will radiate. People are always shocked when I reveal my breast cancer journey, they say, "You don't look like what you've been through." I just smile. I smile, because I live with this story daily, and I'm glad I didn't waste my moments. I didn't waste my time focusing on my cancer. I focused on the moments that I would be cancer free, the moment I would ring the bell from the last chemotherapy treatment. I focused on the moment I could drive my car again, and the day I would return to the work force. I focused on what was next, not what was or had been. The epiphany came to me during the moments I was unmoving, the still moments of recovery in small increments, everyday learning something new about the new me and letting go of the old me. I had to be broken down piece by piece to be re-built. I had one year and two months to focus on me. The woman in the mirror has the same perfect imperfections with a few additional scars. The silhouette is structured with a few nips and tucks, the heart is still big with a lot of love to offer, the unknown released the known, and hope remains constant. The inner voice kept speaking to me loud and clear, **"Don't waste your cancer—Just Live!"**

Acknowledgements

I AM THANKFUL.

To my Husband, and Daughters:

Words will never be able to express what you'll mean to me.

My Love is infinite.

To my Family:

Your support has been the backbone to my recovery.

All my Love.

To my Dearest Friends:

Our friendship knows no limits and the bonds run deep.

Love is patient, Love is kind…and you'll know the rest.

To my WOMC Church Family:

In true extended family, my family and I never went without.

Thank you for feeding us literally and feeding us spiritually.

NICOLE LAWSON-WILSON

To my DST, Inc. Sorority Sisters:

The meaning of Sisterhood has exceeded the definition.

I am forever Grateful.

To my Masterclass writing coach:

Mr. Maximus Wright, I couldn't have done this without your consistent guidance and support.

To Everyone Else:

Please know that any gestures, prayers, acts of kindness, words of encouragement have been received.

I thank each and every one of you from the bottom of my heart.

Center for Restorative Breast Surgery, New Orleans, Louisiana

Drs. Mary Jo Wright, M. Whitten Wise

St. Dominic Hospital, Jackson, Mississippi

USMD hospital, Arlington, Texas (Dr. Kory Jones)

St. Dominic's Cancer Center (Dr. Guangzhi Qu)

The Collage

About The Author

Nicole Lawson-Wilson is a native of Milwaukee, Wisconsin, married, mother of two, residing in Mississippi. Nicole is a graduate of Alcorn State University, Belhaven University and the Institute of Ultrasound Diagnostics. Nicole is currently working in the healthcare field. Nicole is passionate about life, loves all genres of music and hopes to help others facing any life-altering journey with this book.

Connect with the Author

Instagram.com/epiphany_cancerfree

EpiphanyNicoleW1@gmail.com

Leave a Review

If you enjoyed *Epiphany: Don't Waste Your Cancer*, will you please consider leaving a review on the platform of your choice.

Reviews help indie authors find more readers like you-Thanks!

Made in the USA
Monee, IL
04 December 2023

48179415R00049